Divine Timeless Secrets

To An Exceptional Muslim Life

Spiritual Teachings of Quran, Sunnah, Ibn Taymiyyah, Ibn al-Qayyim, and Ibn al-Jawzi to calm your mind and reduce your sadness

Dr. Muddassir Khan

Copyright © 2021

Bismillahir Rahmaanir Raheem.

In the Name of Allah, The Most Merciful, The Bestower of Mercy.

قُلْ أَعُوذُ بِرَبِّ ٱلنَّاسِ ۝
Say, "I seek refuge in (the) Lord (of) mankind,

مَلِكِ ٱلنَّاسِ ۝ إِلَٰهِ ٱلنَّاسِ ۝
(The) King (of) mankind, (The) God (of) mankind,

مِن شَرِّ ٱلْوَسْوَاسِ ٱلْخَنَّاسِ ۝
From (the) evil (of) the whisperer, the one who withdraws,

Preface

All praise is due to Allah. We praise Him, seek His assistance and forgiveness and we seek refuge with Him from the evil of our souls and our misdeeds.

I testify that there is no deity worthy of worship except Allah alone. He has no partner. I also testify that Muhammad (peace and blessings of Allah be upon him) is His slave and Messenger.

This is a short book which explains how the mind works and waswasah (the evil whisperings of Shaitaan). It is based on the teachings of scholars such as Ibn Qayyim, Ibn Katheer, Ibn Rajab, an-Nawawi, Saalih al-Uthaymeen, Saalih Al-Munajjid, Saalih al-Fawzaan (May Allah have mercy on them). It is also based on evidence based Acceptance and Commitment Therapy (ACT). It teaches us how to live a valued mindful and meaningful life while avoiding the plots of Shaitaan and following the straight path of Islam.

This book was written for the person who is desirous of becoming a good Muslim. For the worried, anxious, and depressed Muslim. For the one who is longing to improve himself. For the person who has sinned but wants to repent to his Lord. This book is for all Muslims - the newly converted and for those who have been Muslims since birth.

This book serves as a source of light in the darkness of sins that surround us. You will learn how to experience true faith when you read this book. This book will not only purify your soul but will also teach you how to escape sins. It contains authentic events, advice, and stories that will inspire you to move to the next level in your journey towards the Hereafter.

If you have been desiring to have a loving relationship with your Lord, then this book is written so that you can achieve this goal with ease.

This is not just a self-help book but is a manual of your journey towards becoming a good Muslim. This book will keep your heart from becoming hard and dark. It is a book of hope and forgiveness. You can heal your heart and improve yourself no matter where you have started this journey. This book can serve as a source of your awakening and returning to the Islamic version of yourself.

By reading this compact but comprehensive book with a pure intention and attentive heart, you can cultivate your love for Allah and the Messenger (peace and blessings of Allah be upon him) and live a life of patience, gratitude, and contentment.

How your mind works

A lot of the things we do are things we want to do. So these are deliberate actions. You can choose to pray in the Mosque and this is a deliberate action where you want to earn more good deeds that will help you on the Day of Judgment.

But some of the things we do are done automatically. We don't even have to think about them because our mind does them automatically for us. Automatic actions are often directly controlled by the mind. These include breathing, walking, driving, cycling, and eating.

Actions that are always under our own deliberate control including planning, vacationing, buying a car, the choice of the name of a baby or reciting the Quran.

Some of our actions happen without our thinking about them, or even noticing what we are doing. For example, we can travel a familiar route without making a conscious decision about which direction to turn or how far to go. And we often eat without noticing the taste of food or thinking about what we are eating. Sometimes when someone is talking to us we can be 'turned off', such that what they are saying goes into one ear and out the other. So you *hear* them, but you don't really *listen*. We are on autopilot. When come out of autopilot, we often ask ourselves, 'how did I get here? What did I just eat? What did she tell me?'

The autopilot is ideal for simple actions carried out under normal conditions, but when things are different or dangerous or important, autopilot is not helpful. For example, if we are going down the stairs in the dark, or if someone is giving us vital information, we have to take over the autopilot and be very careful.

An example of an automatic action is to breathe all day. And you probably haven't thought about your breathing once until now. This is because breathing is almost always automatic. We don't need to think about our breathing or do anything to control our breathing, but we can, if we want to.

So now, for just three or four breaths, notice your

breath. Just notice what happens to your body when you breathe in and out. Take control of your breathing for a little while. So gently take a deep breath and breathe out slowly. Most of the time we breathe naturally without thinking about it and without controlling it, but we can notice our breathing if we want to.

If we think and then decide what we're going to do, it is often better for us. If we put in a little effort and think carefully, it often pays to consciously manage actions that are usually performed automatically.

For example, there are two ways to shop. One way is by doing foolish purchases, which are impulsive. They are rushed purchases without thinking. And then there is the conscious buying, which is careful. This is where you match the price with the quality, and this type of shopping will take your time. Mindless shopping involves a lot less effort and it's a lot faster. In other words, conscious shopping is clearly the wiser option.

Your mind is always active. It never goes out. Even when you sleep, your mind continues to function. It makes sure you keep breathing for example and controls what you dream of.

Our mind never goes out, but we often do. When we turn off, people may say that we are lost in our thoughts, carried away by reverie in a world of our own. It is natural for our attention to drift away so that we are often elsewhere. We pray our Salah (prayers) without being aware of the great verses and supplications that we are reciting.

When we dream, we can miss what is happening right now. It is often better not to be miles away, but to pay attention to what is going on here.

There are many benefits to increasing the time we spend focusing on what is currently going on to be present.

The mind often does its own thing and you can't stop it. Think of an apple. It's easy. Now don't think of a pineapple. This we cannot do!

Thoughts are just thoughts

We are not punished for bad thoughts.

The Prophet (peace and blessings of Allah be upon him) said, 'Allah decreed good and bad deeds. Whoever thinks of doing a good deed but does not do it, Allah will account for it one complete good deed. If he thinks and (also) does the good deed, Allah will write it down between ten and seven hundredfold or many more. If he thinks of doing a bad deed but does not do it, Allah will write it down as one complete good deed. And if he thinks and does the bad deed then Allah will write it down as one bad deed.'

The Prophet (peace and blessings of Allah be upon him) said, 'Allah, may He be exalted and glorified, will forgive my followers for what crosses their minds so long as they don't act upon them (the thoughts) or speak of them.'

The thoughts that worry you or trouble you are the evil whispers from Shaitaan. Ask Allah to protect you from such evil whispers.

You cannot stop having these thoughts but should allow the thoughts to pass through your mind without judging them or yourself. You are not a bad person if you get bad thoughts. Shaitaan is causing these thoughts to occur. He wants you to sin. If you fear Allah and don't do the sin, then Allah will write for you a good deed.

Ignoring these troublesome thoughts and not caring about them will help you stop worrying. We cannot control our thoughts but can only control whether we act on them. We will be answerable to Allah only for our actions.

If you get a thought such as, 'What will happen if I start sweating when giving a speech,' you should realize that this is just a thought and not a fact. And in case you do sweat then this is not the end of the world and everyone understands how stressful giving a talk is. You should, therefore, go ahead and give the speech or presentation even if you get these worrisome thoughts.

Such worrisome thoughts are from Shaitaan who wants to disable you so that you don't do any good deed and become lazy and fearful. Being a Muslim your goal is to please Allah and you should do all the good deeds to achieve this goal. Don't let the thoughts from Shaitaan disable you.

Overcautious Mind

The mind is constantly looking for meaning and patterns, even in random material, it is trying to make sense of things. It always wants to know what's going on. The mind often jumps forward. It's not just waiting for solid evidence, but anticipates and speculates on what is likely to happen. And these predictions are often wrong. And they are often very disturbing because the mind tends to think of the worst. So, a minor physical symptom can be taken as indicating a serious health problem or if a family member is returning home late, the mind possibly assumes them to have been involved in a serious traffic accident.

Another important characteristic of the mind is that it automatically reacts to situations and events by triggering particular emotional feelings. The image of the delicious cake makes your mouth water. An image of a dirty ashtray makes you feel disgusted. The image of the snake gives you a sense of fear. You will have some sort of emotional reaction or feelings to images of objects and animals. And it's important to recognize that all of the feelings you had were automatically generated by your mind, you didn't choose or decide to have any of those feelings. They just arrived. It is very important to recognize that feelings are not actions. It is not something that we do.

For the next few seconds, don't think about an elephant. You can think about anything else other than an elephant. If thoughts of a large elephant come to your mind, go ahead and push those thoughts away and don't think about them. You can think about anything else, but whatever you do, don't think about an elephant. This exercise shows you that we cannot suppress our thinking. This is not in our control.

A lot of feelings come to us, whether we like it or not. And because feelings happen to us, whether we like it or not, we shouldn't feel guilty about feelings that arise like anger, resentment, repulsion or jealousy. They just arrived. It is very important to recognize that feelings are not actions. It is not something that we do.

Feelings are like a ball in a pool. When you try to push the ball under the water, the ball keeps popping back up to the surface. You need to hold it and push it to keep it down. It is a struggle that will tire you. Just let go of the ball. It would float near you and you may not like it. But if you let go, your hands become free and you can use them. Enjoy your swim and don't worry about the ball in the pool.

It will help us understand how our mind works if we appreciate our mind wandering. The mind travels in time and space. Our mind is very intelligent, but it is often wrong. Our mind is always looking for threats and avoiding dangers. It is very careful. Our mind is often very critical and is likely to be very critical of us.

Our mind is always trying to keep control. And if we try to take control, it will resist that.

The mental path that the mind creates is sometimes referred to as reverie or thought flow. The particular thought flow created from the millions of possibilities reflects the person's current mood, interests, worries and obsessions. If someone is depressed, for example, their mind will likely follow a dark and pessimistic path. It includes many sad and disturbing ideas and memories.

And the mind of a very anxious person can create a mental journey involving many frightening elements.

Imagine a tomato on the edge of the table. In reality it will stay there without causing anyone any harm. But our mind will always scare us into thinking the worst possible outcome. 'It could easily roll on the ground. Someone could slip on it, if they didn't see it. And if they hit their heads on the stone floor, they could die. This tomato could be fatal.' This illustrates how the mind works. It gets lost along the paths of ideas, and can end up with ominous predictions about what could possibly happen in the future. In this case, the mind turns an ordinary tomato into a deadly threat, and people's minds often lead them down amazing and totally improbable paths.

Schools of thought provide an example of our tendency to overthink a great deal. We live inside our own heads in the world of memories and fantasies rather than in the outside world. There are no worries in the world. Worries only exist inside our heads and we largely live in the past and future rather than the present, but memories of the past and fantasies about the future can produce strong emotional reactions.

Just remembering an event that made you very sad a long time ago can make you sad again now. And just remembering a past incident that was very embarrassing can embarrass you again here.

The wandering mind will often distract your attention from what is happening right now. And it can lead you to places and problems that you find bothersome and painful. What can you do about it? Any attempt to stop the thoughts will almost certainly backfire on you. You can't turn off your mind, and there's not much you can do to distract it. It is therefore better to let it happen. You can notice where your mind is going and accept the thoughts and feelings that arise, but make your own judgments and decisions about what to do.

Waswasah

Waswasah (whisperings of the Shaytaan) is one of the evil methods of the Shaytaan, the whisperer (devil who whispers evil in the hearts of men) who withdraws (from his whisperings in a person's heart after Allah is remembered).

This is always his way: he whispers in the hearts of the people and strives to harm the religious and worldly interests of the believer. This is something that happens to everyone, despite the differences in the extent to which the Shaytaan is able to reach everyone with these whispers, whether they are big or small, whether they are trying to ward off the enemy, until they overcome him and overpower him, or they surrender to him and yield to him.

Muslim reported in his Sahih that 'Abdullah ibn Mas'ood (Allah be pleased with him) said: The Messenger of Allah (peace and blessings of Allah be upon him) said: "There is no one among you except Allah appointed him a companion among the jinn."

They said: "Even you, O Messenger of Allah?" He said: "Even me, but Allah helped me with him and he became a Muslim, so he only tells me to do good."

An-Nawawi (Allah have mercy on him) said:

Regarding the phrase translated here as "he became a Muslim (aslama)", there are two well-known accounts of this phrase. According to one account, the word is to be read as aslamu, which means: "I am immune from his evil and his temptation"; according to the other narration, the word should be read as aslama, which means "he became a Muslim"; what this means is that the jinn-companion has become a Muslim and has become a believer, "who only tells me to do good". Scholars have differed as to which of the two versions is more correct. Al-Khattabi said: The correct version is "aslamu" while al-Qadi 'Iyad thought that "aslama" was more correct because the Prophet (peace and blessings of Allah be upon him) said: "[he] tells me only to do good". They also differed on the meaning of the word "aslama". It has been said that the meaning of the word aslama, translated here as "become a Muslim", is that he surrendered and gave in. In a report reported in books other than Sahih Muslim, the wording appears as faistaslama (he surrendered). And it was said that what that meant was that he became a Muslim and a believer, which is the apparent meaning.

Al-Qadi said: It should be noted that the Ummah unanimously agrees that the Prophet (peace and blessings of Allah be upon him) was infallible and protected from the Shaytaan in his actions, thoughts and speeches.

This hadith indicates that the warning refers to the temptation and whisperings of the qareen (jinn companion); the Prophet (peace and blessings of Allah be upon him) told us that the qareen is with us so that we can protect ourselves as much as possible from him.

The time the Shaytaan is most eager to whisper to a person and take control of him is when he wants to focus on his prayer and worship. Therefore, when Ibn 'Abbas was told that the Jews claimed to have experienced no waswasah in their prayers, he said: What would the Shaytaan do with a ruined heart?!

What you need to do is not worry about whether the Shaytaan's whisperings have come to such and such. Rather, you should strive to get rid of the tricks and whisperings of the Shaytaan and his attempts to take power over you.

Comparison

Even when our mind is focused on what is happening right now, rather than wandering in the past or the future, it will often make a comparison between how things are now and how they were before or how they might have been or how they might be in the future. The process of comparison means that even when things are going great, our mind can use its powers of comparison to find the black cloud in the ray of hope. So even if the current situation is good, your mind might well suggest that it is not perfect. It will not last. It's not as good as it could be. Others are doing better.

Your mind will frequently and often compare you unfavorably to other people or to how you were or how you should be. The general tendency of the mind is to be critical. And pessimistic means that most next-to-the-next comparisons are unlikely to bring us down by suggesting, for example, that you're not as smart as her. You are getting worse. As your friend gets older, he has many more friends than you do.

These days, many people are constantly comparing themselves to others through social media. They get to see everyone having a good time partying, surrounded by friends, and in good shape. Selected material that is published by them in the social media often sends messages such as I am living a good life. I have lots of friends. These edited highlights make for a very distorted picture. A false impression.

If you accept yourself as you are now, you will be much better off. And if your mind compares negatively, just acknowledge that negativity, but also recognize that you don't have to believe everything that your mind says. Your mind tells you that it is very intelligent. The human mind does a lot of smart things while it is constantly working, monitoring what is going on, judging, comparing, predicting, acknowledging. And so we generally accept the judgments of our mind and its suggestions on what to do in a nutshell. We trust our mind, but we have to be very careful about it because our mind is often wrong. And when our mind is wrong, we often suffer. We can show how the spirit sometimes deceives us and plays tricks on us.

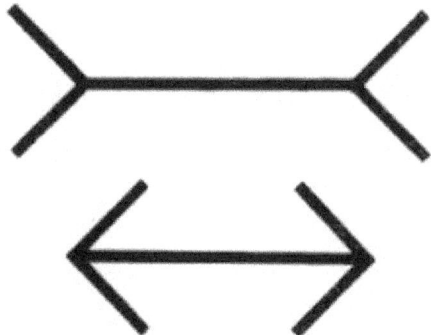

Think about the illusion of simple lines, you've probably seen this a few times before,

And you would probably agree that the upper straight line looks longer, but of course your mind is playing tricks on you because the two lines are in fact exactly the same length. But when you come back to the original image, the illusion is still there. The upper line always looks longer, even if you know it isn't.

Sometimes your mind will send you a message that something is dangerous when you absolutely know it is safe. And if you know, there's no real danger, go ahead and do it, even if your mind is cautioning you. Even if it's scary.

If you know that you already have locked the door, for example, don't go back and check it again and again, even if your mind tells you to check it one more time, just to be safe. So act on what you know, rather than on the irrational and unwarranted ideas and feelings that your mind has generated. It is the wise and sensible thing to do.

Here's another example, you absolutely know that a friend's pet snake is perfectly harmless, and you'd like to touch it. Your mind can tell you that the snake is horrible, disgusting, and dangerous. So what would happen? Would you like to go ahead and handle the snake or the warnings in your mind?

While the warnings in your mind can always cause you anxiety, you know that it is really safe and that it would be wise to go ahead and deal with the snake. This idea is captured in a saying you may have heard before - feel the fear and do it anyway. It is very important to recognize that you do not have to believe everything your mind tells you or follow its ideas. So be skeptical of what your mind is saying. You should treat it with a healthy disrespect. And when there is an important decision to be made, be careful but be wise.

Shaitaan is our enemy

Allah informed us of our enemy, Iblis (the Shaitaan). When He asked him why he refused to prostrate to Adam, Iblis maintained that he was better than Adam. He asked Allah to allow him respite, and He allowed him.

Then Iblis, the enemy of Allah, said, "Because you have led me astray, surely I will wait against them (on) Your Straight Path. Then I will come to them from before them and behind them, from their right and their left, and you won't find most of them to be grateful." (Al-A'raf 16-17)

The majority of interpreters of the Quran explained that the response of Shaitaan was in an orderly manner to show his determination to conspire against the believers.

The Straight path

Ibn 'Abbas (Allah be pleased with him) said: "The Straight Path is the clear religion of Allah (Islam)."

Ibn Masud (Allah be pleased with him) said: "It means the Book of Allah (the Quran)."

Jabir bin Abdullah (Allah be pleased with him) said, "It is Islam." And Mujahid said, "It's the truth."

These are all expressions for one meaning, which is the path to Allah.

Sabrah bin Al-Faakah (Allah be pleased with him) related that the Prophet said: "Shaitaan is waiting for the children of Adam, using all his (devious) ways."

Ibn 'Atiyyah reported that Ibn' Abbas said regarding (then I will come to them from before them), that Shaitaan would try to influence the children of Adam "in their worldly affairs". Ali bin Abi Talhah related that the above verse meant: "I will make them doubt their hereafter." This was in keeping with Al-Hasan's narrative which referred to Shaitaan's attempt to make them (the believers) deny the Resurrection, Heaven and Hell.

Mujahid said: "(Then I will come to them from before them) means, from where they will be able to see (his evil temptations)."

(and behind them); Ibn 'Abbas said: "It means: 'I will make them desire their world of illusion very much.'" Abu Salih said: "It means: 'I will make them deny the hereafter and distance them away from it.'"

Ibn 'Abbas also said it meant "I will make them doubt the importance of their Religion (Islam) and their good deeds." Al-Hasan said it meant, "I will make them refrain from doing good deeds."

{and from their left} Al-Hasan said: "It means, 'I will command them to do bad deeds, which I will make so attractive before their eyes."

Ibn 'Abbas has been authentically reported as saying: "Shaitaan did not say (from above them) because he knew that Allah, the Exalted, is above them."

Ash-Sha'bi said, "Allah has bestowed His mercy on them from above."

Qatadah said, "Shaitaan has come to you, O son of Adam, from all directions except from above. So, he could never prevent you from achieving the mercy of Allah.

Al-Wahidi said: "Some say: 'The right represents good deeds, while the left represents bad deeds', since the Arabs say: 'Place me on your right, but do not place me on your left', which means: 'Make me among your closest, and not among your most distant.'"

Al-Azhari reported, citing other scholars, that Shaitaan made an oath with the Dignity of Allah.

Iblis said: By Your Might, then I will surely mislead them all. (Sa'd 82)

Shaitaan tries to mislead them all, so that they deny everything that has been reported about the outcome of previous civilizations and the issue of resurrection, and also confuse people in their daily activities.

Other scholars like Abu Is'haq and Az-Zamakhshari,

(and the word is that of Abu Is'haq) have said, "All these directions have been mentioned for the greater emphasis, that is : 'I will come to them from all directions'. It could mean, and Allah knows best, 'I will make sure they are being misled on all sides.'"

Az-Zamakhshari said interpreting the verse: "I will come to them from all the four directions, where the enemy usually comes from." This is an example of his (the devil's) whisperings and the extent of his influence over them. Allah said in another verse, addressing Shaitaan: "Stir any of them with your voice, and rally your cavalry and infantry against them." (Al-Isra 64)

Shaqiq said: "Every morning Shaitaan lies waiting for me in four places: in front of me, behind me, my right and my left, and says: 'Do not be afraid, for Allah is the most forgiving, the most merciful.' Then I recite (the Quranic Verse): "And verily I do forgive one who repents, believes, and does righteous good deeds, and then remains steadfast in doing them." (Ta-Ha 82) When Shaitaan comes from behind me, he wants to make me worry about the people I will leave behind (when I die), so I recite: "And no moving (living) creature is there on earth but its provision is due from Allah." (Hud 6) When Shaitaan comes to me from my right, he comes to stir up my desire for women, so I recite: "The blessed end is for the pious." (Al-A'raf 128) And when he comes from my left, he comes to stir up all my desires, so I recite: "And a barrier will be set between them and what they desire." (Fatir 54)

Ibn Qayyim said, "Man follows one of the four paths, and none other; either he takes a path to his right, to his left, in front of him or behind him. On each path, he finds Shaitaan waiting for him. If man follows any of these paths, while keeping Allah's commandments, he finds that Shaitaan poses obstacles for him to prevent him from being obedient to Allah. But if man follows one of these paths for committing sins, Shaitaan will encourage him and provide for everything the support he needs."

The following verse supports the comments of our pious scholars, as Allah said: "And We have appointed for them (devils) intimate companions, who have made fair-seeming to them, what was before them and what was behind them." (Fussilat 25)

Al-Kalbi said explaining this verse, "We assign to them a few companions among the devils to them."

Muqatil said: "We have prepared for them companions among devils."

Ibn 'Abbas said: "What is before them (these are things of the world), and what is behind them (eternal things from the Hereafter)."

The meaning is, "They made this world look just (and fair-seeming) to them, until they preferred it to the hereafter, and even called them to deny it (the hereafter) completely."

Al-Kalbi said, "They made fair-seeming to them what was before them - affairs of the Hereafter", - that there is no Heaven, no hellfire and no resurrection, "and what was behind them - matters of this world" - their straying (misguidance) in this life.

Ibn Zayd said: "They made all their past bad deeds, and those to come, appearing to them righteous." (that is, the devil made what they were doing of the sins look so attractive to them, that they did not repent and never intended to give up the evil deeds that they were ready to commit).

When Shaitaan, the enemy of Allah said: "Then I will come to them from before them and behind them"; he meant in this world and the hereafter; and when he said: "From their right and their left"; he meant "the angel of good deeds, on the right, exhorts his person to do only good deeds, so the devil should approach him from this side to prevent him from doing so; while the angel of evil deeds on the left forbids him to do them, then the devil should approach from that side to encourage him to do so. All of this is summarized in the following verses:

"By your might, then I will surely mislead them all." (S'ad 82)

"They invoke only female deities besides Him (Allah), and they invoke nothing but Shaitaan, a persistent rebel. Allah cursed him. And he (Shaitaan) said, 'I will take an appointed portion of your slaves. Verily, I will mislead them, and surely, I will arouse in them false desires and certainly, I will order them to cut off the ears of the cattle, and indeed I will order them to change the created nature by Allah.' And whoever takes Shaitaan as a protector (or helper) instead of Allah, has certainly suffered a manifest loss. He makes promises to them and arouses in them false desires, and Shaitaan's promises are but deceit." (An-Nisa 117-120)

Ad-Dahhak said (the verse means): "An assumed portion is a known proportion of the slaves of Allah."

Az-Zajjaj said (it means): "A proportion that I have appointed for myself."

Al-Fira 'said (it means): "The people over whom he (Shaitaan) was made to have authority; so it's like the assumed proportion."

Ibn Qayyim said, "The reality of the hypothesis is that it is an estimate, which means that whoever follows Shaitaan and obeys him, becomes among the proportion of people appointed by Shaitaan, which will become his share." For, the people are divided into two sections: the followers of Shaitaan and the followers of Allah's guidance.

"Then I will surely mislead."

far from the truth, and

"surely I will awaken false desires in them and certainly."

Ibn 'Abbas said: "Shaitaan intends to hinder the path of repentance."

Al-Kalbi said (it means): "Shaitaan will arouse in them false desires and false certainties, that is, there is no paradise, no hellfire or resurrection."

Az-Zajjaj said (it means): "He combined leading them astray with arousing in them false desires so that they have no fortune in the Hereafter."

It has also been interpreted as: "I will stir up in them the urge to follow sinful desires and innovation in religion."

And it was interpreted as: "I will awaken in them the

desire to hold on to the pleasure of this world, until they prefer it to the hereafter.

"I will order them to cut off the ears of the cattle"

cutting off Al-Baheerah's ears - and this is the word of the majority of Quran interpreters. Scholars said it was also a reference to piercing a child's ear, which some of them allowed for adornment of a female child only, supporting their opinion with the Hadith of Umm Zar', narrated by 'Aishah, Allah be pleased with her, in which she said, speaking of Umm Zar's husband, Abu Zar' : "He has given me many ornaments and my ears are heavily laden with them." The Prophet said to Aishah, Allah be pleased with her, after she recounted the above Hadith: "I am yours as Abu Zar is to Umm Zar'." (Al-Bukhari)

Imam Ahmad had authorized this for a girl but not for the boy.

"and indeed I will order them to change the nature created by Allah"

Ibn 'Abbas said: "Shaitaan meant the religion of Allah", and this is the opinion of Ibrahim, Mujahid, Al-Hasan, Ad-Dahhak, Qatadah, As-Sudday, Sa'id bin Al-Musayyib and Sa'id bin Jubayr.

It means that Allah created His servants with a healthy nature, that is, Islam. Allah said:

"So direct your face firmly towards the Religion (Islam), as a pure natural believer, the natural pattern of Allah (Fitrah) upon which He made mankind. There is no change in the creation of Allah. This is the true religion, but most people do not know it. Turn (in repentance) towards Him (only), and be afraid and be dutiful to Him." (Ar-Rum 30-31)

The Prophet said, "No child is born except with Al-Fitrah (Islam), and then his parents make him Jewish, Christian or Zoroastrian. Also, when an animal produces a perfectly formed young one, do you see part of its body cut off? Then he (peace and blessings of Allah be upon him) recited, "The natural pattern of Allah (Al-Fitrah) upon which He made mankind." (Bukhari)

The Prophet linked two issues: changing someone's Fitrah causing a child to become a Jew or a Christian, etc.; and changing the creation of Allah through cutting. These are two things that Iblis (Shaitaan) said he was going to do; he therefore changed the Fitrah of Allah using polytheism, and changing their naturally created form (as defined by Allah).

"He makes promises to them and arouses false desires in them."

His promises are the ones that reach our hearts, such as: "Your life could be extended, so that you will realize all your desires in this life. You could achieve a high status, above your own people and your enemies." In this way, Shaitaan increases hope, making false promises and arousing false and diverse desires in one. The difference between what he promises and what he arouses is that he promises lies and arouses unattainable desires. The low and corrupt self always feeds on Shaitaan's false desires; it likes to live on false hopes.

"Shaitaan threatens you with poverty and commands you to do fahsha (evil deeds); while Allah promises you forgiveness from Himself and bounty." (Al-Baqarah 268)

It is said, "Shaitaan commands you to commit fahsha", (i.e. to be mean and stingy) (as in this particular verse). Muqatil and Al-Kulabi have been quoted as saying, "The term fahsha' in the Quran means illegal sex, except in this context where it means miserliness."

The correct opinion is that the term fahsha' in its general sense refers to each type of fahisha (evil act). It refers to an action not mentioned, so the attribute carries the general broad meaning of the word.

Therefore, we say that Shaitaan commands mankind to do bad deeds and among them miserliness. Allah has mentioned, in the above verse, both the threat of Shaitaan and his commands. He orders them to do bad deeds and threatens them with bad consequences (if they do good deeds).

These are two things Shaitaan demands of man: he warns them not to do good deeds, so they refrain from doing them; and he commands them to do evil deeds which he makes righteous to them, and so they easily indulge in them.

Allah then mentioned His promise, if He were to be obeyed, by those who follow His commandments and avoid His prohibitions; for which his promise is his forgiveness and generosity. His forgiveness is a protection against evil, while his generosity (bounty) is the offering of good.

Abdullah bin Mas'ud reported that the Prophet said, "Shaitaan exercises his influence over the son of Adam, just like the angel. The influence of Shaitaan is that he holds the promise of evil and the denial of truth. And the influence of the angel is that he holds the promise of good and the affirmation of the truth. Thus, whoever perceives this (good promise) must praise Allah and whoever finds it contrary must seek refuge with Allah from Shaitaan, the cursed one. He then recited this verse: "Shaitaan threatens you from the prospect of poverty and invites you to be indecent." (At-Tirmidhi)

The angel and Shaitaan take turns with a person's heart like the alternation of night and day.

Mind and Safety

The mind is very careful because our mind has evolved to keep us safe. It is always on the lookout for any possible threat, but minds tend to be too sensitive. They can become alarmed too easily and can worry and frighten us when there is no real danger. Our minds hold us back telling us that the world is a dangerous place. 'Stick to things, you know, don't take chances'. The mind focuses very much on threats and things that could go wrong. The mind tends to be very careful, better safe than sorry. So it is trying to stop us from doing anything new, adventurous, or daring. If we listen to our mind, we'll just stick to the things we know, in the same places, the same activities and the same people. We limit ourselves to things that are familiar and sure.

Our minds are often very critical and negative, focusing on the things that are wrong or that can go wrong. They find opportunities to criticize just about anything that can be criticized. Minds are always looking for any sign of weakness or failure. And when they find something, they think it's not quite right, they focus on it and magnify it. The mind's extreme critical bias can be particularly distressing and damaging when it focuses its criticism on us. Our mind will often make negative judgments about our parents, for example, or about our personality, habits, or social behavior. If your mind seems to have it going for you in terms of being critical to you, rest assured that you're not the only one who thinks that almost everyone is critical and cruel to them. Sometimes, you certainly can't rely on your friendly mind. Our minds can bombard us with criticism that undermines our confidence. "No one really likes you. You have always been selfish. You have no will, you are a total failure."

So what does your mind usually tell you when you look at yourself in a mirror? Does it say you look good? Your eyes are beautiful? You still have that big smile? Or does it say things like you look really messy - just look at those wrinkles. Another really bad hairdressing day! Such insulting reviews can be very upsetting, but only if you take them on board and treat them seriously. If you just notice the criticisms in your mind and let them be, it will take away their power to hurt you.

Besides being very critical, the mind is also authoritarian. It will try to organize you around its opinions. It often tries to dictate what we should and should not do and how we should react. It says to you, "You should be working a lot harder. You shouldn't waste your time. You should defend yourself."

If you decide to do something that your mind doesn't want you to do, it will do its best to discourage you. "It is simply unnecessary. It will never work. It is very risky. You would just be wasting your time again." We often do what our mind usually suggests without giving it much thought, but it's important to recognize that we don't have to accept the mind's suggestions, advice, warnings, or commands. Your mind does not have the power to control what you do. Ultimately, you are in control of your actions. So when your mind suggests something, or advises or bullies or tells you that you owe something, you are free to choose to follow your suggestions or do whatever you want to do. Remember this.

We have the power to change the relationship we presently have with our mind. We can decide things are going to be different from now on. You should become a cool watcher of your mind so that you just notice what it is doing without being too much controlled or absorbed by it. You should realize that there is a distinction between you and your mind. They are not the same things. You are not your mind.

For example, your mind travels here and there and back and forth in time. But you, the observer, are always there in the present. You can observe your own thoughts and feelings. You can see as your mind rises to imagine all of your thoughts and feelings as if these are aspects of a performance. It would be a lot of action on stage because there is a lot going on in your mind and you can see what is going on. So where are you? You are not on stage. You are the audience, a spectator, who only notices what your own mind is doing. So there is you and there is your mind. And these are separate. You are not your mind.

Let's do a simple exercise of mindful breathing. It involves spending a little time just noticing all the sensations that occur when you inhale and exhale.

Avoidance and Change

It's tempting to avoid situations that make you feel sad, embarrassed, or afraid. And it's tempting to try to suppress unwanted thoughts and feelings, but people often make things worse and hurt more by trying to avoid situations or by struggling or putting their lives on hold until things get right or are improving. It's often best to be prepared to come to terms with hardships that can't be changed and negative feelings that you just can't turn off.

There are some things you can change and some things you can't. Imagine that you are waiting at the station for a train and the train is delayed. There is absolutely nothing you can do to make the train arrive faster. So what's the best thing to do? Well, you can go up and down the platform. You can keep looking at your watch, or you can complain to the railroad staff or read a book or magazine, maybe phone a friend for a nice chat, or just look at people or clouds, or you can meditate. This is just one of the many things we can't control. Others include the weather, the actions of others, the family we were born into, and many aspects of our health. It is very important to recognize that there are things that we just cannot change. If we accept these things we will have peace.

It's important to recognize that a key thing that we can't change at will is the way we feel, but that doesn't stop people from telling us to just control our feelings, to cheer us up. They will tell us, "Forget it, pull yourself together, don't be disturbed." If we try to directly control our feelings, we are doomed to failure. We cannot turn our feelings on and off. Since we can't control our feelings, struggling to suppress feelings is futile. And it's often exhausting and it often makes it worse.

Direct attempts to overcome pain or to overcome depression or to stop worrying or to fall asleep are all likely to make things worse.

If you were to come across quicksand, what would your natural reaction. You would be struggling really hard to get out of it. But what effects would that have? You could find yourself sinking quickly. This natural panic reaction could be fatal. If you want to survive fast sand, don't do what comes naturally. The best thing to do is to float on the sand fast. It will definitely hold you down, and then you can roll gently down to solid ground. It is certainly not the natural reaction, but it could save your life.

Often past flashbacks increase our suffering. The same is true of unwanted thoughts. Trying to get rid of them often increases their strength and frequency at all.

Everyone has extreme, disturbing, and unwanted thoughts that come to their minds from time to time. It is often very disturbing and shocking. People are often very distressed by the content of their intrusive thoughts. They may fear that having such thoughts is very unusual, could lead to extreme actions, indicate a hidden desire, or reflect their true self. All of these ideas are wrong, but they often lead to feelings of guilt and distress. Of course, people do whatever they can to try to get rid of those thoughts and to try to keep them from coming back. But trying very hard to reduce these thoughts is exactly the wrong thing to do. These efforts will generally strengthen the power of unwanted thoughts. When you are trying to suppress an intrusive thought, it is more likely it is to become strong. If instead of struggling to suppress a disturbing thought, you simply accept it, then before long, the thought will be gone. If you just accept unwanted thoughts as well as unwanted feelings and urges and leave them alone, they will just disappear like bubbles. They will disappear naturally. The thought will simply disappear.

So when you have unwanted thoughts, notice them, accept them, let them be, but don't get caught up in them and try to suppress them. Rather than struggle to conquer or eliminate the thoughts and distressing feelings, which is likely to make matters worse, make the decision not to struggle but to allow those thoughts and feelings to be there. In other words, practice *acceptance*.

When thinking about the experience of pain, it is helpful to distinguish between pain itself and suffering. It is often possible to reduce the level of suffering even when the pain level itself cannot be reduced. When you are in pain, the natural response is to do whatever you can to end the pain. For example, you can try pain relievers or physiotherapy or maybe even surgery. And if one of these is successful and gets rid of the pain, that's fine. But what if you can't get rid of severe pain and have to live with it in this situation, some people continuously focus on the pain and struggle more and more to fight it. They just won't give up.

There are two different strategies for dealing with persistent pain, focusing on the pain and fighting it or accepting the pain and continuing as usual. Which of these two strategies you think will result in less suffering. If you try to fight the pain, the pain will fight back. As a result, your efforts to control pain will actually increase your suffering. All of your hard work would have backfired and made things worse for you. So fighting the pain will often increase your suffering. Partly, that's because focusing on the pain means you'll be paying a lot of attention to it. So you will think about it and you will often feel it more.

But focusing on other things pushes the pain to the edge of your attention. Additionally, when people try to deal with pain, they often contract their muscles. The increased tension is likely to increase the level of pain and suffering. Some people find temporary pain relief by using various distraction techniques. But these are really types of avoidance. These are quick fixes that only provide short term relief, whereas acceptance can have a lasting effect when there is no medical treatment capable of relieving the pain. The best way to reduce suffering is to accept the pain and carry on as much as possible, doing things that make life interesting and enjoyable. It means living with the pain and not letting the pain put your life on hold.

So struggling to overcome pain often increases the level of suffering. And the same goes for emotional pain. Struggling to control your depression is likely to make you more depressed, and struggling to let go of unwanted thoughts is likely to increase the frequency and strength of those thoughts. Trying very hard not to worry is likely to worry you even more, and trying to overcome unwanted urges will often make them stronger. So, in addition to the distress and suffering that comes directly from a problem such as physical pain, depression, worry, or intrusive thoughts, we often create additional distress indirectly through our reactions, and how we are responding to these issues. So, our reactions to problems often make matters worse and aggravate our suffering. Thus, we often inflict significant additional costs on ourselves.

For example, if we ask someone who is severely depressed about how his depression affects him, he can point out two major additional costs of depression. He can tell that because of my depression, I don't go out socially and I don't exercise. This means that the total aggregate costs of depression include depression and not going out and not exercising. But even if his depression persists, he could still go out and exercise. And if he managed to get out socially and he managed to exercise, then his overall costs of suffering would decrease. He would still feel the pain of his depression, but he would not suffer more because of the additional costs.

It is therefore important to appreciate the difference between the direct effects of a problem and its overall impact. And it is often possible to reduce the overall impact, even if the original problem remains unchanged. When you have a painful problem, which cannot be fixed, it is better accept it and carry on rather than constantly struggle to solve the problem or put your life on hold.

Some people have this attitude, "I have a problem that

needs to be resolved, and there's no point in trying to get on with my life until I am fully well." Someone who takes this attitude says, "I will start living my life again on my own when I stop caring about things or when I got my confidence back or when I'm no longer depressed". But there a much better approach - just go on with your life. Don't put your life on hold while you wait for all of your problems to be resolved, since accepting and continuing with life will minimize the impact of the problem. On the other hand, struggling to repair or remove it will often increase the impact and increase the suffering.

Imagine that you own a bus and earn a living by driving the bus. Naturally you drive along the road and at each bus stop you let the passengers get off and you pick up anyone who wants to get in. Most of the passengers are fine. They behave well. They present no problem. But some passengers are a real nuisance. They make a lot of noise and are often rude and aggressive. You really wish they weren't on your bus and you hope it won't be long before they get off.

So these are the passengers of the bus scenario. What are the main issues raised by this simple story? You are the driver and the trip is the journey of your life. The passengers of the bus, the good guys and the bad guys and the things going on in your head, are all those thoughts, feelings, memories, images and cravings that you will have in your life. A lot of them are nice or neutral, but some distract and bother you. These can include worries and scary images, and you would really like to get rid of them. So what are you going to do about those unwanted thoughts and feelings, about these problem passengers? Some drivers would focus entirely on difficult passengers and think about possible strategies to get rid of them. Similarly many people focus all of their attention on their anxiety, physical pain, disease, or depression. They try all the ways possible to make them go away.

Some drivers decide to stop the bus and announce that this bus is not going anywhere until some people get off, but that probably won't do any good. Unwanted passengers don't just get off the bus and can get mean, making the situation worse. So, a driver who struggled to force the horrible passengers off the bus might well come to regret it, and then wish that they would just accept the situation and continue with the journey.

Some people stop their bus. They put their lives on hold as they keep trying to get rid of problem passengers, such as anxiety or depression. They put all of that energy into dealing with their issues which can be very exhausting. They would be much better off if they only concentrated on continuing their journey. In other words, they should live with their problems while they lead a full and interesting life as much as possible.

In addition when trying to solve a problem that cannot be solved people often try to alleviate their suffering by using *avoidance*. The obvious way to not be bothered by a scary or embarrassing situation is to simply avoid it. "I am very anxious to go for a dental exam." The obvious thing to do in this situation is never take the medical exam. "I am embarrassed to meet new people." The obvious thing to do is stay away from people you do not know. "I still feel panic when I travel by bus." The obvious thing to do is never travel by bus. Now, such avoidance can bring immediate relief from anxiety, and it may seem like the answer, and the sane thing to do. But it is not. Avoidance leads to even further fear about the situation and strengthens your belief that such situations need to be avoided.

Instead of avoiding such irrational fearful situations, you can work to overcome the fear by committing yourself to deal with the situation, object, action, or person that triggers your irrational fear. To give yourself the best chance of overcoming your irrational fear, you have to face the thing you fear, confront the object or situation you dread, and accept that when you do this you will feel fear and anxiety. And so you feel the fear and do it anyway.

Avoiding or escaping from a scary, embarrassing, or depressing situation will immediately reduce the negative emotion such as fear, but it will reinforce the fear, thereby fueling the problem, and maybe even making it worse. As the fear or embarrassment gets worse, the avoidance strategy will be used repeatedly, thus beginning a vicious cycle.

We often do things to avoid or escape our own painful emotions. So, when we are scared, or in a bad mood, anxious, embarrassed or worried, we can use various strategies to escape the feelings that we cannot bear. It would be much better if we accepted these negative emotions and lived with them rather than trying to avoid or escape them. But almost everyone uses quick resolution strategies to try to avoid or escape negative feelings. These range from everyday behaviors to actions that can be quite extreme. These quick solutions can include overeating, drinking, smoking, illegal drugs, social withdrawal, overspending, impulse buying, and gambling.

This does not mean that you should avoid the good and clean things that Allah blessed you with to help you reduce your problems and worries. You can indulge yourself and give yourself a boost when the pressure is on and you feel the tension. And it's clear that sometimes a chocolate really does the trick. The danger is that you can come to depend on eating, drinking, smoking, drugs, or gambling as your usual means of escaping negative feelings. The effects of quick fixes are usually short lived and the tactic will usually need to be repeated very frequently.

We often make things worse for ourselves by trying to fix things that can't be fixed and trying to avoid situations, thoughts and feelings that we find painful. But coming to terms with things that we can't control, accepting the situation is often a better way for us to reduce our distress. This is the state of acceptance that will make us free from worries. In this state you allow yourself to feel all the emotions, whatever they are, and you let yourself think any thoughts, even if they are disturbing.

Devilish insinuations of Shaitaan

One of Shaitaan's ploys is to whisper to Muslims about ritual cleansing (such as ablution) and Salaah, when they intend to perform them. He manages to prevent them from following the Sunnah of the Prophet by making them believe that all the teachings of the Sunnah are not sufficient to worship Allah correctly; so they try to invent other methods, hoping to increase Allah's reward, when in fact they reduce it or even cancel it altogether.

There is no doubt that it is Shaitaan who calls people to follow bad thoughts and temptations; they are wicked people who obeyed Shaitaan, accepted his call, and followed his command. They rejected the Sunnah of the Prophet to the extent that someone believed that even if he performed ablution like the Prophet and washed like him, he would still not be able to clean himself properly.

The Prophet used to perform Wudu '(ablution) with a

quarter of the Syrian ratl (around 3.202 liters of water), and washed his body with a ratl and a quarter. A person who is under the influence of the inspiration of the devil would see this measure as not even sufficient to wash his hands.

It has been authentically reported that the Prophet performed the steps of ablution one by one, and would not go beyond three times for a particular step. He even mentioned that, "Anyone who goes beyond this has transgressed and acted unjustly." The person under the influence of Waswasah is a transgressor, as the Prophet testified. Therefore, how can we come closer to Allah with acts that transgress beyond His limits?

It was also reported that the Prophet (peace and blessings of Allah be upon him) practiced Ghusl (the main ritual ablution of the whole body) with 'Aishah (Allah be pleased with her) using a single large bowl, in which traces of dough remained. If the person, under the influence of Shaitaan, heard of someone doing the same, they would oppose them by saying, "This is not enough for two people to wash properly!"

The Prophet (peace and blessings of Allah be upon him) used to wash himself using a large bowl not only with 'Aishah but with his other wives, such as Maimunah and Umm Salamah (Allah be pleased with all of them).

Ibn 'Umar was also quoted as saying, "During the lifetime of the Prophet, husbands and their wives used to perform ablution using a single bowl."

The Prophet's guidance states that it is permissible to wash from a container, even if it is not full of water; and whoever washes only if the basin is full of water and does not let others share it with him, is in fact transgressing the Sunnah of the Prophet

Shaykh Ibn Taymiyah (Allah bless him) said, "It takes more force to rebuke such people for legislating beyond Allah's divine legislation; because they worship Allah with their innovations, not by following the Sunnah of His Prophet."

This authentic Sunnah confirms that the Prophet and his companions did not waste water by pouring it abundantly, and it was also the practice of their disciples.

Sa'id bin Al-Musayyib (Allah bless him) said, "I used to perform ablution from one vessel, and left some for my wife."

Imam Ahmad (Allah bless him) said, "A knowledgeable person should only use a small amount of water."

When the Prophet performed ablution or washed his whole body, he used to put his hand inside the container to obtain water; he rinsed his mouth and washed his nose. The person under the influence of Shaitaan's whisperings would not agree; he would most likely consider this water unclean and would never share a container with his wife! He would feel disgust at this thought, as the disbeliever feels when the name of Allah is mentioned.

People under the influence of Shaitaan's whisperings may say, "We are taking these precautions for our religion; implementing the words of Prophet: 'Leave what makes you doubt and turn to what does not make you doubt', (Recorded by Imam Ahmad) and 'Whoever saves himself from suspicious things, saves his religion and his honor', (Al-Bukhari) and 'A sin is that which weaves in someone's heart.'

Some scholars of the past have said, "A sin leaves the heart perplexed and anxious." The Prophet passed a fallen date on the way and said, "If I was not afraid that it was from a Sadaqah (charitable donations), I would have eaten it." (Al-Bukhari) The Prophet abstained from eating the date as a precaution.

Imam Malik gave a fatwa (legal opinion) regarding a person who divorced his wife and had doubts, whether it was the first or the third divorce pronouncement, that it should be considered the third pronounced divorce, as a precautionary measure to avoid any illegal sexual relationship (between the man and his divorced wife).

He also gave a fatwa concerning a man who divorced one of his wives but forgot (that he had divorced her), that all his wives would automatically be divorced from him, as a precaution against his forgetting; a preventive measure against doubt.

If a man says to his wife, "At the end of the year you will

be completely divorced (three times)" then she should be divorced from him immediately (that is, by the time he says so), as it is a preventive measure.

The scholars also said, in this context of precautionary measures, that whoever misses the stain of impurity in his garment, must wash it completely.

The scholars said that if a person wears clean clothes and one of the clothes should become unclean, but he is in doubt as to which it was, then he can perform the Salaah by wearing a garment over the unclean garment (depending on the number of unclean spots), and perform an additional Salaah for greater certainty; to ease his conscience.

Scholars have said that if clean vessels are mixed up and mistaken for unclean vessels, one should avoid them all and practice tayammum instead. Also if one is confused about the direction of the Qiblah, then one should perform four Salaahs according to some scholars, to relieve one's conscience with certainty.

They said, "Anyone who does not perform a particular

Salah in one day and forgets it (which Salah), should perform the five Salah for that day again."

The Prophet ordered that whoever has doubts in his Salaah, should make decisions based on certainty (i.e. act according to his certainty). He prohibited Muslims from eating game if it was not known whether the prey had been hit by him or by someone else, and also if it fell into water.

These are some examples of the long subject of doubt and precaution.

Precaution and action according to certainty are not rejected in Islam, although some like to call it Waswasah.

If we take precautions for ourselves and act only according to our certainty, leaving behind what makes us doubt, and turning to what does not make us doubt, and avoiding suspicious things, we certainly would not be outside the teachings of Sharia, nor will we indulge in the world of bid'ah (innovation). This is better than taking things for granted, acting recklessly, regarding one's religion, such as not paying attention to how much water one uses for wudu', or where one performs the Salaah, or the purity of his clothes; such a person does not care about suspicious things and considers everything as pure, even if it is doubtful.

They said, "All they object to us are the precautionary steps we take to perform an obligation or avoid a prohibited one. It's better than acting carelessly towards both; because this often leads to breaches of obligations and involvement in prohibited things."

Allah said, "Indeed, in the Messenger of Allah you have a good example to follow for one who hopes for Allah and the Last Day, and remembers Allah much." (Al-Ahzab 21)

"Say: If you really love Allah, then follow me, Allah will love you." (Al-Imran 31)

"And follow him so that you may be guided." (Al-A'raf 158)

"And verily this is my straight path, so follow it and do not follow other paths." (Al-An'am 153)

The straight path that Allah commands us to follow is that of the Prophet who was followed by his companions. Whatever deviates from it, it is a form of transgression. Nevertheless, the transgression can be serious or less serious; and in between there are levels of transgression which can only be measured by Allah.

Therefore, the scale with which one can use to identify righteousness from transgression is the Sunnah of the Prophet and his companions.

A transgressor can be unjust (an oppressor), a Mujtahid (A legal jurist formulating independent decisions in legal matters), or a Muqallid (a person who blindly imitates others). Some of them deserve either punishment or forgiveness, but some of them may even be rewarded once depending on their intentions and efforts in worshiping Allah.

The Prophet's guidance as practiced by his companions shows which of the two paths is best to follow.

One should remember the prohibition of going beyond

one's own limits and extravagance in Islam, and that observance of the Sunnah is the central objective of the Deen (Religion).

Allah said, "O People of the Book, do not exceed the limits of your religion." (An-Nisa 171)

"And don't waste by extravagance." (Al-An'am 141)

"These are the limits ordained by Allah, so do not transgress them." (Al-Baqarah 229)

"Do not transgress limits. Truly, Allah does not like transgressors." (Al-Baqarah 190)

"Call on your Lord with humility and in secret. He does not like aggressors." (Al-A'raf 55)

Ibn 'Abbas said: "In the morning of Al-Aqabah, the Prophet said to me, as he was mounting his camel, 'Pick up some stones for me.' So I picked up seven stones for him. He then started to shake them in his hand and said, 'Such people (who go beyond Allah's limits) you should aim at.' Then he said: 'O people, beware of excessiveness in religion; for people before you were destroyed by their excesses in religion.'" (Ahmad and An-Nassai)

Anas said: "The Prophet said, 'Do not impose austerities on yourself so that austerities are imposed on you. For people who have imposed austerities on themselves, Allah has imposed austerities on them; their survivors are to found in cells and monasteries. Then he quoted: Monasticism, they invented it, we did not prescribe it for them.'" (Abu Dawud)

The Prophet (peace and blessings of Allah be upon him) forbid austerity or severity in religion, going beyond what is prescribed in Islam. He also informed that a person's austerity over himself is the cause of Allah's austerity on him, either by qadar (divine decree) or by sharia' (Islamic law).

Austerity by Sharia' is when someone imposes severity on himself, with a heavy commitment, and commits himself to it.

Austerity by qadar is when someone is under the influence of Shaitaan's whisperings.

Al-Bukhari said, "People of knowledge did not like excess in wudu', and going beyond the practice of the Prophet. Ibn' Umar said: 'Performing ablution correctly is purity.'"

Therefore, fiqh - all aspects of fiqh - is economy in religion and adherence to the Sunnah.

'Ubay bin Ka'b said, "Follow the Path and the Sunnah (of the Prophet); for every servant of Allah who follows the Path and the Sunnah (of the Prophet) remembers Allah, and his body shivers for fear of Allah. His sins would be taken away as the leaves are wasted away from their dry tree. Saving (economizing) in the path or a sunnah of the Prophet is better than an individual interpretation in a particular dispute in the Sunnah. So make sure that your economy in your activities is in line with the practice of the Prophet."

Sheikh Abu Muhammad Al-Maqdisi said in his book "Dham Al-Muwaswiseen":

"All praise be to Allah who guided us with his blessings

and honored us with Muhammad and his message. He helped us to follow the Sunnah of His Prophet and made a sign for the Love and Blessing of Allah to be bestowed to us."

"Say, 'If you really love Allah, then follow me, Allah will love you and forgive you your sins. And Allah is Often Forgiving, Most Merciful.'" (Al-Imran 31)

"And My Mercy embraces all things. I will order it to those who are pious, who give Zakat and believe in Our Signs; those who follow the Messenger, the Prophet who can neither read nor write." (Al-A'raf 156-157)

"So believe in Allah and his Messenger, the Prophet who cannot read or write, who believes in Allah and his words, and follow him so that you may be guided." (Al-A'raf 158)

In truth, Allah has made Shaitaan an enemy of man; he waits against him in the right path, and comes to him from all directions and paths, as we have been informed by Allah

"Because you have led me astray, I will surely stand against them on Your Right Path. Then I will come to them from before them and behind them, from their right and from their left, and you will not find most of them grateful." (Al-A'raf 16-17)

Allah has warned us against following him (the devil) and ordered us to be his enemy and adversary; He said: 'Surely Shaitaan is an enemy to you, so take him as an enemy." (Fatir 6)

"O children of Adam, do not let Shaitaan fool you as he got your parents out of paradise." (Al-A'raf 27)

Allah informed us of what Shaitaan did to our parents (Adam and Eve) in order to warn us not to obey him and to invalidate any excuse if we choose to follow him. He ordered us to follow his right path and forbade us to take different paths. He said, "And verily, this is My Straight Path, so follow it, and do not follow other paths, for they will separate you away from His Path." (Al-An'am 153)

The Right Path of Allah is that followed by His Prophet

and the Companions. Allah said, "Ya - Sin. By the Qur'an, full of wisdom. Truly, you are one of the Messengers, on the Straight Path." (Ya-Sin 1)

"Verily, you are indeed on the right guidance." (Al-Hajj 67)

"You are indeed guiding to the right path." (Ash-Shura 52)

Thus, whoever follows the Path of the Prophet is on the Straight Path, and is one of those whom Allah loves and forgives their sins. And whoever departs from the actions and words of the Prophet is an innovator, a follower of the Path of Shaitaan, and not among those to whom Allah has promised rewards and mercy.

People who are under the influence of Shaitaan's whisperings are likely to obey his commands, and reject the Sunnah of Prophet and his companions. Their blind obedience to Shaitaan leads some of them to believe that if they perform Wudu and Salaah in the manner of the Prophet their Wudu and Salaah would be invalid.

They also believe that feeding children in the Prophet's way and eating together, in a group, from a plate (the way Muslims eat their meals in general), would contaminate the meal, making it unclean.

Shaitaan's control over these people caused them to blindly obey him. It is similar to the school of Sophists who deny the facts of creation and things which are perceptible to the senses. They even deny man's knowledge of himself, in matters of certainty and necessity. Such people wash themselves, recite with their tongues, listen with their own ears, but still have doubts about their actions; whether they did or not! Shaitaan even makes them doubt their own intentions, which they certainly know, deep in their hearts. Instead, they accept Shaitaan's whisperings, which they did not intend for Salaah, for example, to argue against their own certainty. All of this is an exaggeration in their obedience to Shaitaan and the acceptance of his Waswasah; thus anyone who attains this level of obedience to Shaitaan has obtained total obedience to him.

A person under the whisperings of Shaitaan accepts the words of the devil, harming himself, sometimes by immersing himself in cold water, or opening his eyes under cold water, washing them until they become painful.

Abu Al-Faraj bin Al-Juziy reported from Abu Al-Wafa 'bin' Uqayl that a man told him, "I dive into the water several times and still doubt whether I have washed myself properly or not, so what is your opinion?" The Sheikh said to him: "Go, for the obligation of Salaah is withdrawn from you." He said, "Why do you say that?" The Sheikh replied, "Because the Prophet said, 'There are three people whose actions are not recorded: a madman whose mind is disturbed until he is restored, a sleeper until he wakes up, and a boy up to puberty'; and anyone who dives in water several times, but has no doubts whether he is wet or not yet, is a madman."

Ibn Qudaamah added: "Shaitaan occupies the minds of these people until they miss the moment of doing Salaah in congregation, or keeps them busy doing 'niyyah' (intention) until they miss the time of the First Takbeer (the saying of the first Allahu Akbar after the Imam, at the start of the Salaah), or even miss an entire Rak'ah or more.

It has been reported to me that a man, who was strongly influenced by the whisperings of Shaitaan, was extremely obsessed and anxious to express his niyyah before performing a Salaah; one day he repeated the word "I pray" and "Salaah of such and such" repeatedly.

Shaitaan has indeed succeeded in tormenting certain people in this world before they reach the Hereafter; he prevented them from following the Sunnah of the Prophet, so that they became people of extreme and excessive religious practices, while they think they are doing good.

Anyone who wants to get rid of this ordeal must believe, with certainty, that the truth is to follow the Sunnah of the Prophet in his words and actions. We must be sure that we are on the right path, and that any other path is only a seduction of Shaitaan, in the form of his diabolical whispers. We must know for sure that Shaitaan is his clear enemy, who only attracts someone to evil deeds; as Allah said:

"He only invites his disciples to become the inhabitants

of the blazing fire." (Fatir 6)

He should give up all that is opposed to the Sunnah of the Prophet and not doubt that Prophet was certainly on the right track, and that anyone who doubts such a fact would indeed become a non-Muslim and a disbeliever. One should look at the way in which the Companions and the Tabi'in (disciples who came after the Companions) who followed the Prophet in his Sunnah, and should imitate them; for one of them said: "There were people (Companions) before me, that if they did not wash beyond their fingernails, I would not have washed them beyond them;" it was Ibrahim An-Nakha'i.

Zin Al-'Abidin once said to his son: "O my son, give me clothes to wear when I answer the call of nature; because I saw flies landing on dirt, then touching clothes afterwards." Then he observed that neither the Prophet nor his companions used to wear more than two garments, so he canceled his request.

Whenever 'Umar bin Al-Khattab was determined to do something, and then was told that the Prophet had never done such a thing, he gave up the idea. Once he said, "I am considering giving up wearing these clothes because I have heard that they are painted with urine from the elderly!" then Ubay asked him: "Why are you giving it up? For the Prophet used to wear it, as well as his contemporaries, and if Allah had known that it was illegal, He would have made it clear to His Prophet." So 'Umar and replied, "You are right."

It should be known that none of the Companions was under the influence of Waswasah, because if the latter (waswasah) was a virtue, Allah would not hide it from His Prophet and from the Companions who are Allah's most favorite creation. If the Prophet had lived in this time, he would have hated them (those who follow the whisperings of Shaitaan), and if they (followers of Shaitaan) had lived in the time of Umar, he would have punished them.

Acceptance

Practicing acceptance on a regular basis will give you greater power of acceptance when it could be of great use to you. For example, if you suffer from chronic physical pain or extreme emotional distress, developing your power of acceptance is like working out in a gym in order to build muscle strength. When faced with tough and painful situations, if you have developed acceptance strength, then this strength could be of much use.

You don't have to just live with your suffering and this is not acceptance. It is just the opposite. The point is, acceptance without a struggle is often the best way to reduce suffering. You do take actions that you possibly can to reduce the pain and suffering. But even if with all the possible actions if you continue to feel pain, then you accept and go on living a productive life based on your values.

In general, the words react and respond have the same

meaning, but it can be useful to make a clear distinction between them. Reaction is an automatic reflex, uncontrolled and driven by impulse and emotion. Responding is more conscious and deliberate. It involves careful thought. Impulsive reactions often lead to reckless actions and increased suffering. Whereas a conscious mindful response will often result in more sensible actions and a lot less distress.

What will a Abdul do when he feels like he wants to watch a movie? If he reacts impulsively then he will go watch the movie. However, if he responds mindfully, he will think how this will increase his sins and cause the displeasure of his Creator. He will therefore decide to not watch the movie.

In many situations it is better to respond rather than react and often leads to wiser, healthier, and a beautiful Islamic outcome, and a better quality of life. Reaction to something will usually lead to the same action over and over again, but responding to it involves considering various possible options, so it adds flexibility.

Thinking about different options increases the chances

of doing something different. If you just watch a movie and never think about it, why would you change? But thinking about your sins might be a step towards changing your habits.

Even when the external situation remains exactly the same, our response can change a lot. We can completely change our response even if things don't change. For example, something that you found very exciting, you might now find it boring, not because it has changed, but because you have changed. You are bored with it. In the same way food that you once considered disgusting, you now judge it delicious because your taste has changed.

Our response to a particular situation, person, disease, or activity can completely change because we change.

Zaheer used to not like going to the mosque. He wanted to always watch cartoons and play video games. But when he understood the great number of good deeds he would earn if he went to the mosque, he started to love and enjoy going to the prayers.

Jamal learned about patience and contentment in Islam. The awful pain that he used to feel even after treatment has now become bearable when he decided to accept his situation and become a patient Muslim. The pain has not changed, his response to it has changed.

Halimah once used to get distressed because of the evil thoughts that used to occur to her. When she understood them to be the 'Waswasah' from Shaitaan, she did not pay any attention to these thoughts. They now come and go in her mind without her feeling guilty or ashamed. She has understood that her thoughts are involuntary and not 'her'. Her thoughts have not changed, she gets them even now frequently, but she has changed.

Umar (Allah be pleased with him) hated the Prophet (peace and blessings of Allah be upon him) and the religion of Islam, but that hatred soon turned into a fierce love for the Prophet (peace and blessings of Allah be upon him) and Islam.

So, the ultimate responsibility of our actions lies with us. If someone drinks at a party, he should blame himself and not the party. If someone runs away whenever he sees a lizard, he should not blame the lizard. You are responsible for your response. You have the power to chose your response. You can run away from a party where Haram drinks are being served and save your soul from the fire of Hell. You also have this option! You don't have stay in a place of evil.

You should always do what needs to be done without paying much attention to your involuntary thoughts and feelings which can be from Shaitaan. Frequently without much thinking (mindlessly) we allow our current feelings to dictate what we do. We want to snack, we have a snack. We don't feel sociable, we avoid people. We feel tired, we stay in bed. But in many cases, we know that these actions are not the best thing for us to do. When we recognize that our actions are driven sometimes by the evil thoughts and feelings caused by Shaitaan, we can decide to step in and take control. We can then consciously determine what we think is the best thing to do Islamically as a Muslim, and then commit to doing it. So we make a careful judgment on the best thing to do, even if that's not what we feel like doing right now. And then we are firmly committed to doing what we worked out is best for us in the Hereafter.

I don't feel like going to work today, but I realize that this is just a feeling. Shaitaan wants me to be lazy. I really can't afford to lose this job.

I don't really want to go for this check-up, but I'm going, because I know it's the right thing to do.

I really want a drink, but I'm going to avoid alcohol from today because I have come to know that Allah does not want a Muslim to drink.

So you don't have to be in the mood to do what needs to be done. And you don't have to be in a good mood to do the right thing. And you don't have to feel motivated to act motivated. You decide based on the Quran, authentic Hadeeth, and the rulings of scholars as to what is the best thing to do. And sometimes that means you feel the fear and you do it anyway, or you feel the lack of motivation, but you do it anyway, or you feel the urge to sin, but you don't do it anyway.

Things will probably turn out a lot better for you if your

actions are motivated, not just by what you want to do, but according to what Allah wants you to do!

A good way to become more aware and conscious is to put it into words, writing it down, talking about it with someone or to talk about things with yourself. Deliberate self-talk and self-analysis can help your resulting actions become more Islamic. Some people think it's crazy to talk to yourself before doing an action. This is certainly not true. Talking to yourself can help you see things clearly and find the best thing to do. Sometimes it makes a lot of sense to speak to yourself aloud. When you talk to yourself, it slows things down, helps you think clearly, and helps you come up with different ideas about what you may do. Ask yourself, 'what I as a Muslim should do in this situation?'

And all of these aspects will help you respond carefully rather than just reacting. The effects of talking to yourself, depend on what you say and how you say it. Don't insult yourself, be positive. Be kind to yourself. Don't be discouraged, be encouraging, and speak to yourself in a friendly voice. Talk to yourself as a good friend trying to be helpful and encouraging. Be kind in what you say to yourself. Be your own best friend.

A very important message to take away from this book is that you don't have to do what your mind suggests you to do or tells you to do or tries to order you to do! But we often forget about this and just let our minds control our actions. To prevent this from happening we have to be steadfast and sure of ourselves, and energetic, and we may have to become a rebel. As a rebel, be careful of the times when your mind is clearly very eager for you to do something, then consider doing the opposite. For example, if your mind says to you: 'Don't pray the optional prayer, the fard is sufficient', then pray the optional prayer and an additional prayer as well. And if your mind says, 'Oh, don't speak up and tell them about the Quran since they can make fun of you and criticize you', speak out loud, make your point and feel happy that you have taken control. Remember, you don't have to listen to your mind's warnings, and you don't have to follow its instructions or orders. You just have to do what Allah and His Messenger (peace and blessings of Allah be upon him) want you to do.

Your actions are in your control and you decide what to

do. So when someone or your own mind tries to persuade or order you to do something, you are free to do it or not to do it, make your decision. So when it comes to actions, you don't have to do what your mind or someone else tells you to do. You don't have to do what you are told. How liberating is that? Ultimately, you are in control of your actions and it can help you live a better and more fulfilling life by taking control and determining what you are going to do carefully, decisively, and mindfully. You've probably done what almost everyone does, doing what comes naturally, reacting spontaneously, following your instincts and being guided by your mind. You may have struggled for a long time trying to fix things you don't have the power to solve, and trying to ignore, avoid the problems that really bother you. It's not your fault if all of your efforts haven't been successful in making things better. You might feel exhausted and wonder if you have the power to improve your life. A Muslim is positive and hopeful that things will get better. If you stop struggling and accept your problems for what they are, then you will feel liberated. You can ignore your distressing thoughts and feelings and move forward. It is the path of acceptance and commitment.

Mindfulness is the ultimate way to experience the fact that you are not your mind. Mindfulness involves you noticing what is going on in your mind.

There is a world of difference between descriptions and evaluations or opinions. But in many cases the mind makes the big mistake of treating them as the same, with the result that we often also become confused. If I read a book and tell someone it was really funny, I'm not really describing the book itself. I describe my reaction to the film. So I should really say that I found the book very funny. Someone else might say the same book was boring or stupid, and neither of us would be right or wrong. We are all entitled to our own opinion. There is no truth to whether a particular book is funny or boring. Likewise, if we say the man is eighty years old, that is the description. But if we say that the man is intelligent, it is an evaluation. And if we say the writer is Indian, that's a description.

Many descriptions you give of yourself, apart from your name, age, address, are really evaluations, which have been possibly invented by your critical pessimistic mind. You may think that you are stupid, fat, boring, etc. These are only evaluations not factual.

Imagine two people, both fifty years old. One of them thinks, 'I am old'. The other things that I am young. Both their thoughts are neither good nor bad. They are an evaluation, but these different evaluations just might affect how they feel and how they act. If someone asked you what kind of person are you, you might just be at a loss for words. However, your mind give an answer with a whole range of assessments. Some of them could be very negative and very critical of you.

This mind presents its evaluation as if it is a fact. So rather than just suggesting that you are stupid (which is only the mind's opinion), the mind would be insistent that you are stupid (it would no longer present its opinion as an opinion). 'And that's a fact', the mind says with confidence, leading you to think, 'I'm stupid. I am ugly. I'm fat, I'm not worth anything. I am a coward. I am insensitive.' None of these are ever true or false because they are description, personal opinions, and personal evaluations. So don't believe your mind where it tells you what you really are like, be warned that it is just making it up. Your mind is entitled to its opinion and you are entitled to yours. Your mind can be negative and criticize you over a lot of things, but you can balance that out by being positive about yourself, choosing what opinions you have about yourself.

Prayer

The evil whispered during prayer and at other times comes from the Shaytaan, who is anxious to lead the Muslim astray and deprive him of the good and keep him away from good. One of the Sahabah complained to the Messenger of Allah (peace and blessings of Allah be upon him) about waswas during the prayer, and he said: "The Shaytaan comes between me and my prayers and my recitation, confusing in that. The Messenger of Allah (peace and blessings of Allah be upon him) said, "He is a devil called Khanzab. If he affects you, seek refuge with Allah from him and spit dryly to your left three times. He (the Sahabi) said, I did it and Allah took him away from me. (Reported by Muslim, 2203)

Good concentration (khushoo) is the essence of prayer. Prayer without good concentration is like a body without a soul. Here are two of the things that help develop the right focus:

1 - Endeavor to reflect on what you say and do,

meditating on the meanings of the Quran, dhikr (words of remembrance) and du'as (supplications) that you recite; keeping in mind that you are conversing with Allah as if you can see Him. For when the worshiper stands to pray he is speaking to his Lord, and ihsan (perfection of worship) means worshiping Allah as if you saw Him, and knowing that even though you cannot see Him, He sees you. Whenever a person experiences the sweetness of prayer, they will be more inclined to do it. It depends on the level of his faith - and there are many ways to strengthen his faith. This is why the Prophet (peace and blessings of Allah be upon him) said: "Of the things of your world, women and perfume have been made dear to me. and my joy is in prayer."

2 - Strive to ward off things that may distract you during prayer, namely thinking about things that are irrelevant or distracting. Waswas affects each person differently, because waswas has to do with the level of a person's doubts and desires and the degree to which a person is attached to other things or fears other things.

Allah says (interpretation of meaning):

And if an evil suggestion comes from Shaytaan, seek refuge with Allah. Indeed, He is the hearing, knowing. (Fussilat 36)

Some of the Sahabahs complained about the waswas bothering them. Some of the companions of the Messenger of Allah (peace and blessings of Allah be upon him) came to the Prophet (peace and blessings of Allah be upon him) and said to him: "We find in us thoughts which are too terrible to speak of." He said, "Do you really have such thoughts?" They said, "Yes". He said, "It's a clear sign of faith." (Reported by Muslim).

Al-Nawawi said in his commentary on this hadith (prophetic tradition): "The words of the Prophet, 'It is a clear sign of faith' mean, the fact that you think it (Waswasah) as something terrible is a sign of clear faith, because if you do not dare to pronounce it and you are so afraid of it and to talk about it, let alone believe it, it is the sign of one who has reached perfect faith and who is free from doubt."

And it has been said that this means that the Shaytaan

only whispers to those whom he despairs of tempting, because he is unable to tempt them. As for the kafir (non-Muslim), he can approach him however he wants and is not limited to waswas, he can play with him as he sees fit. Based on this, what the hadith means is that the cause of waswas is pure faith, or waswas is a sign of pure faith.

The fact that you hate it and your heart recoils from it is a clear sign of faith. Waswas happens to all who turn to Allah while reciting the dhikr, etc. It is inevitable, but you have to be firm and patient, and persevere with your dhikr and your prayer, and not give up, because in this way you will push back the plot of the Shaytaan. Indeed, Shaytaan's plot has always been weak. Whenever a person wants to turn to Allah, waswas reminds him of other things. The Shaytaan is like a bandit: whenever a person wants to go to Allah, he wants to block the way. Therefore, when one of the Salaf (pious predecessors) was told that the Jews and Christians say, "We do not experience waswas," he said, "They are telling the truth, for what would the Shaytaan do with a ruined house? (According to Fatawa Shaykh al-Islam Ibn Taymiyah, 22/608).

The cure:

1 - If you feel that this waswas affects you, say: "Amantu Billahi wa Rasoolihi (I believe in Allah and His Messenger)." It was reported from 'Aishah that the Messenger of Allah (peace and blessings of Allah be upon him) said: "The Shaytaan comes to one of you and says, 'Who created you?' And he said "Allah." Then the Shaytaan said, "Who created Allah? If this happens to any of you, let him say, Amantu Billahi wa Rusulihi (I believe in Allah and His messengers). Then it will disappear from him." (Reported by Ahmad, 25671; classified as hasan (sound) by al-Albani in al-Saheehah, 116).

2 - Try to stop thinking about it as much as possible and keep busy with things that distract you from it.

Reality of Thoughts

Your thoughts, feelings and worries are not real things in the world, like houses, dogs or cars. They are not just in your head. If we truly appreciate this, we would never be upset with any thoughts or feelings. If I think I might ever get cancer, it's just a thought that has no bearing on whether or not I get the disease. This thought doesn't make it more likely or less likely. So, such thoughts do not reflect reality, but they can still bother us. A lot. Of course, it would be perfectly reasonable for me to feel anxious if I ever received a medical diagnosis of a serious illness. But that is very different from me being worried, just because my mind came up with this thought that I have cancer or will develop cancer sometime in the future!

Unfortunately, people are often extremely distressed with thoughts about problems and medical conditions that they don't have and never will. Here is another example of confusing the thought of something with the real thing. Suppose I am shopping one day and suddenly the thought occurs to me that I might steal something from the store. Stealing is a great wrongful action in Islam. But in this case I did not steal and I just got the thought that I will steal. It would be a big mistake on my part to feel that I did something wrong almost like I really stole something. I have to understand that the idea of stealing just happened to me. And that it's just a thought. Thoughts are just thoughts. We can have a thought and take note of it without believing it or acting on it.

Having a thought that comes to your mind is something that happens to you. It is not something you do. If you ever feel embarrassed, anxious, or guilty about a thought like shoplifting it means that you are making the mistake of confusing a thought with reality, in this case confusing the mere thought of stealing with the actual act of stealing. A thought that comes to you is not a plan or an intention. It's just a thought. And just as we have to understand that thoughts are only thoughts, we also need to understand that dreams are just dreams. Having a dream is not an action we take. A dream is happening to us. If you ever feel embarrassed or guilty about something you dreamed of, you are making the mistake of blaming yourself for something that is out of your control. It's just something that happened to you.

We often confuse thoughts and reality. This type of confusion or error is known as fusion or merging. We can use various strategies to overcome such a fusion. And these are known as Defusion techniques.

Compare these two statements. "I am a loser, and 'I think' I am a loser (which may not be true and is just a thought my mind has produced)". The second statement recognizes that the thought that I am a loser is just a thought. So if your mind is triggering thoughts like I'm really stupid or I'm no good, just remember the reality of the thought. By adding this sentence, 'I think' I'm really stupid. This is one of the effective defusion strategy.

Another defusion technique is known as constant repetition, where you simply repeat the word over and over again, until it temporarily loses its meaning to you. The word simply becomes a sound stream. You can feel this diffusion effect by practicing the strategy anytime. Just repeat any short word, like paper or apple or failure, over and over again, for 30-40 seconds, paper, paper, paper, paper, paper, paper. You will find that after a while the meaning of the word goes into the background and the sound itself comes to dominate. This constant repeating broadcast strategy can also be used to neutralize words that you find very scary.

Remember the old saying: sticks and stones can break my bones, but words will never hurt me. Is there any truth in what is said here? Well the first line is right, sure sticks and rocks can break your bones. But what about the second line? Have people ever been hurt by words? Oh yes, they sure are. Sticks and stones can hurt you all the time, no matter what you think of them, but words will only hurt you if you believe they are real. If you understand that words are just sounds or just marks on paper and you just accept them like that, then they hurt. Otherwise these words will never hurt you.

Remember that the mind's confusion between words and reality is just one example of merging or fusion. Another confusing form of fusion, is confusing the image of an object with the object itself. An example of this would be to become hungry or salivate when we see an image of some delicious food. In such a case, we would react to a printed image or a screen image as if it were real food, as if it was edible. Merging can also involve confusion between what is going on in our mind and the outside reality. And we often make the big mistake of confusing me and my mind. But you are not your mind.

The ultimate defusion activity is mindfulness. Mindfulness involves the person noticing that their thoughts and feelings are separate from themselves.

Mindfulness technique: Floating Leaves on a Moving Stream.

This technique involves you actively, but in a very gentle way, by separating yourself from your thoughts. With a little practice, you can use this technique to reduce the distress caused by particular thoughts and feelings. This activity won't stop you from having unwanted thoughts or make them go away, but it will help you respond to unwanted thoughts and feelings in a way that makes them less disturbing. So let's start this activity with leaves floating on a moving stream.

Get into a comfortable position and close your eyes if you are happy to do so. Now imagine that you are sitting by a river, watching the water slowly flowing downstream. Imagine that is a warm sunny day that you were alone and you were calm and relaxed watching the river slowly go by. And as you are looking at this, you notice that there are a few tall trees, slightly upstream, and sometimes a big leaf falls from one of the trees that slowly glides through the air until it lands on the surface of the water. And then the river gently carries the leaf downstream. Watch it happen. Watch the leaves fall into the water, slowly pass in front of you before being transported further downstream until they disappear from view.

As you imagine this scene, various thoughts may come to your mind. You can have memories of past events, or thoughts about the future. Some of these thoughts can be worrying, or happy, or sad. When a particular thought catches your attention, imagine placing it on a leaf that floats downstream, transferring the thought directly to the leaf as a picture maybe, or maybe as a word or message written on the leaf. So stay in that steady position over there on the bank, watch the leaves go. If a thought comes to you gently place it on a leaf and observe as the leaf carries it downstream and ends up passing out of sight.

Let it happen naturally, when you notice what is happening. If you are distracted by noise or feeding into your body, notice that too and let it pass. If at any time you get distracted from the activity, gently walk back to the riverside and the flowing river.

So now let's spend a minute or so doing this activity in

silence. Imagine the scene, the river, the trees, the occasional fall of leaves. And place your thought as an image on one of the floating leaves.

It is worth practicing this defusion technique regularly and spending more time on the imaginary bank. Perhaps for as long as 10 to 15 minutes. Floating leaves on a moving stream can be a very useful way to distance yourself from agonizing thoughts, images, and feelings. And over time, you can really benefit from the simple yet powerful defusion activity.

To pay attention and being mindful is essential to a healthy life. A lot of our actions are mindless and foolish, and generally that's okay. It's a good job that we usually don't have to think about our breathing or how to move our legs when we walk. These things are usually automatic. They operate on autopilot. Once we have learned to walk, read and drive, we no longer have to think about how to perform such actions. We just do them. Our mind does them automatically. However a lot of the things we do, they require us to pay attention, to think carefully, and to sort things out. In other words, being aware and mindful. There are two ways to be aware. If you were to buy a car, for example, you would think about it very carefully. What is the price? Is it the right size? How many gears does it have? Does it have good brakes?

You would never buy a car without thinking about it. You weigh things and then make a careful decision. You would do it in full awareness and mindfully. So working on things, weighing things, thinking about the future, making judgments and making deliberate choices and decisions, is one way of being aware and mindful. But another different way of being aware is what we call mindfulness. This involves only noticing what's going on. Not to deliberately think about things, to make judgments or to sort things out, but simply to notice what is happening here right now. And now when you practice mindfulness, you can focus on something that is going on out there, like the waves on the seashore, or your focus may be internal so that you notice bodily thoughts or sensations. Mindfulness does not involve changing your mind or changing what you think, but it does involve changing the way you respond to your thoughts and your feelings so that you just notice your mental processes in a gentle, curious, and detached way.

Dealing with your thoughts and feelings in that way allows you to stay focused in the present moment. Just noticing means you're not trying to change or control what's going on. You just effortlessly notice when you practice mindfulness. You notice and accept what is happening without engaging in any judgment or evaluation. So when a thought arises, you are not concerned whether it is right or wrong. You just don't go there.

Mindfulness helps us understand that all of our thoughts and feelings, including those that annoy us or frighten us, are but brief events. They will leave soon. Don't make the mistake of thinking that mindfulness is primarily a relaxation technique. You can be relaxed when practicing mindfulness, but you can just as easily be active and tense. For example, if you practice Kung Fu mindfully. Mindfulness is not a state like trance or hypnosis. Mindfulness is not a state of mind, it is the activity of simply noticing, of noticing what is going on inside and outside in a gentle, curious and detached way.

Let us do a brief mindfulness activity. Focus your attention on one part of your body. For example focus on your left hand, get into a comfortable position and close your eyes if that's okay with you. Shift your attention to your left hand, making sure it's in a position that you can comfortably hold for the next two to three minutes. When you're settled in, start focusing on any sensations you can feel in that hand, and just focus on those sensations for a little while. Maybe you can send some heat or some cold to your left hand. Perhaps there is a hint of discomfort, fatigue or numbness. Maybe you can feel a slight tingling or a little shaking. By focusing on your left hand, you might also become aware of the sensations in other parts of your body. If thoughts arise, notice them and allow them to be there.

These thoughts will simply disappear. And so now for a short while, focus on any sensation that you can feel in your left hand.

Mindfulness and sleep.

When we can't sleep at night, we can lie in bed and try very hard to fall asleep, but trying very hard may continue to keep us awake. On the other hand, if we accept that we are awake and stop trying to fall asleep, we can really relax. And if that happens, guess what? We might well fall asleep.

People who regularly practice mindfulness often sleep less, but feel refreshed and alert when they wake up. Mindfulness therefore seems to offer some of the benefits that people normally get when they get a good night's sleep. So if you are awake, when you don't want to be awake, it is good to practice mindfulness. It can make you calm and help you sleep. And if you don't sleep, you might be reaping some of the mindfulness benefits you would get from sleeping. So, anyway you gain by practicing mindfulness.

One context of practicing mindfulness is meditation, but mindfulness can be practiced in many other less formal ways as well. Almost anything can be done mindfully in full consciousness. There are many quick and easy ways to add some mindfulness to your life. And if you practice them regularly, they can do good. Informal mindfulness activities, includes mindful walking, mindful stretching, keen observation of the waves on the shore.

Watch the clouds carefully, consciously move. Mindfully stand in line waiting. Mindfully and consciously drink a glass of water. Have you ever spent time watching clouds move across the sky, or noticing fish swimming in an aquarium, or watching raindrops run down a window, or just staring at the stars in the sky? Any of these activities of just noticing counts as informal mindfulness attention activity.

People who regularly practice mindfulness can experience many benefits, including lower stress levels, a greater sense of calm, fewer depressing thoughts, and better focus. They may also experience less suffering when in pain, increased body awareness, better sleep and increased creativity. Regular practice of mindfulness is also associated with less impulsivity and greater self-control. Mindfulness leads to increased self-compassion. Benefits of practicing mindfulness regularly are numerous and it is a possible way to have a less stressful life.

A Valued Life!

Your personal values relate to the things that are important to you. Values are the things you really care about. But how do you know what your values are? How to find out what you value and how to make sure your actions and lifestyle align with your values. Making a commitment to act in accordance with your values and then keeping that commitment is the best way to feel that your life is on the right track, that you are doing the right thing, that you are doing the best you can. These are the issues that we will address in this final film.

You might remember the passengers from the bus story. Well, here's that bus again! It's your bus. You are the driver. Now the question is where do you want to take your bus? Where do you want to go in your life? Most bus trips have a fixed destination, but life isn't about going somewhere. Life is the journey itself. Nonetheless, it is good to have a clear direction for your journey. Some bus drivers seem to move around without clearly knowing where they are going. 'I'm not going anywhere in my life'. And some seemed to be going in circles. 'I never get anywhere. I always come back to the same old place'. But some drivers seem to know exactly where they want to go. Their journey has a clear direction making their journey more meaningful and fulfilling.

The route (your valued life) in the chosen direction may not be smooth. You can expect a number of dangers and various delays on the road. Various life events can distract you from the chosen route and you can even get lost completely for a while … before getting back on track. Other people may try to steer you away from your chosen direction, but don't let other people or your own mind dictate what you must, or should do based on your values. This is your trip. It's your life. The best direction for your trip is in line with your personal values, the things you care about, the things that really matter to you, the things that give your life meaning. But it is not always easy to know what are our values. To recognize what is really important to us if we ask someone directly, what are your values? They would probably look at us weirdly and shrug their shoulders.

To identify your own values and choose your values, you should be guided by your feelings. When something feels right to you, it indicates one of your values. And when something feels wrong it also indicates one of your values. The stronger your values, the more you care about things. If you didn't value anything, nothing would make you happy, nothing would make you sad, and nothing would make you angry.

Whenever you are angry, your anger reflects something that is close to your heart. So this points to one of your values. If you say I get angry when my kids make a mess, it shows you value cleanliness or order. If you feel happy with yourself, because you arrived early, it indicates that you value punctuality. And if you say with pride, I spent hours weeding the garden, which suggests that you enjoy working hard. So think about these questions. What makes you feel warm and why? What is it that really irritates you and why? What are you proud of and why? What makes you sad, and why?

You can also use various thought experiments to help identify your values. One of them is, 'they are talking about me'. Imagine that you are on the phone to a friend, but due to a technical problem, you can hear your friend talking to someone else who knows you very well, and you quickly realize that they are talking about you . Of course, you are very interested in what they have to say about you. So you keep listening. What would you most like to hear about yourself?

The things you would most like to hear will reflect your values. So if you'd like to hear any of them say, Adil is always ready to help anyone. It shows that you value generosity or kindness. And if you'd like to hear any of them say, Adil is always so excited about things. This suggests that you would like to be seen as enthusiastic, indicating that enthusism is one of your key values. And if you want to hear a friend say, Adil always sees the glass half full. It would show that you value optimism and positivity.

Another useful way to identify your values is to recognize any strong feelings you have about people you know. There will be some people you really love, and knowing why you love them, will help you identify one of your values. But you can really hate some people and finding out why you don't like them, will also highlight one of your values. So, as a brief activity, think of someone, maybe a friend, relative, or neighbor that you have positive feelings, such as feelings of respect or admiration. And now think about why you have such positive feelings towards them. What do you really like to respect or admire about them? The answer to this question is likely to identify one of your key values. And now think of someone you have negative feelings for. Feelings of aversion, or anger or disrespect. Why do you have negative feelings about this person? And what value does that relate to? If you become aware of a strong feeling towards a real or fictional character, when you are reading a book, take the opportunity to identify one of your values. Ask yourself why I really like that person? Or why do I hate this person? This can help you identify your values and then can help you live your life according to your values.

We generally experience life as more satisfying and meaningful when our lifestyle reflects our values, the things we really care about. This applies to all aspects of our life, including our relationships, our hobbies, our work, and even the programs we watch on TV. And when you're about to make key changes in your life, it's good to look at them based on your values. This can help you make the best decision about which direction to take.

When you do something in accordance with your core values, you generally feel that it is the right thing to do. While it may also seem difficult and demanding. Your values will often trigger painful emotions. For example, if the one of your key values is kindness, then hearing about acts of cruelty might make you sad or angry. But feeling angry at the cruelty can make you do something to end that cruelty. People's values are often reflected in the charities they support. And in political parties they vote for. Actions based on values often call for courage. The person may need to go the extra mile.

Commitment

Lead a truly fulfilling life. Your actions should reflect your values. You have to do what's right for you.

But it's not always easy. Things can get in your way. When you've decided on the correct thing to do in line with your values, you have to commit to doing the best, even if it is very difficult. After taking a decision based on your values, the next step is commitment. And even if it hurts, if you've made a commitment to do something that will be very difficult or uncomfortable, you might just have to go for it.

But what if you have a weak moment and don't respect your commitment. For example, someone who has been on a diet to lose weight may have a weak moment and eat a few chocolates or drink a soda drink. If this happens, they may decide that their attempt at dieting has failed completely and quit the diet altogether. Or, a person who is quitting smoking may have a single cigarette and then decide that their attempt was unsuccessful and they are going to start smoking again. And that will then give them a great excuse to go out and buy a big pack of cigarettes. So a lot of times when someone makes a commitment and then they break that commitment, then they will give up on the commitment, and they can even go one step further and give up any commitment, especially if their mind is saying, 'Oh, well that proves that you just did have no will', and they believe it. If you make a commitment and break it, the best thing you can do is to make the commitment again, and you may have to do it again and again.

Very few people who end up quitting smoking are successful in the first time they try. For example, on average, smokers were successful in quitting on their fifth or sixth attempt. It is not easy.

How do people react to a setback? Sometimes a disappointment can take us a long way. After a setback, you have to make a realistic and careful judgment of the situation. Is it better to continue and try again? Or does it make more sense to quit? The wisest thing to do is to consider the different options and think about them carefully. The types of setbacks people often experience in their lifetimes include disappointing progress in school, failure to lose weight, difficulty establishing a close relationship, unwanted ending of a close relationship, refusal to being accepted for a course or a job, and financial hardship and loss. Sometimes, you may be aware that your mind is trying to undermine you by telling you that you will never do it. 'It will never work, you might as well give up now', your mind may say to discourage you. You should recognize that negativity in your mind and make a firm commitment, to do your best to be successful.

According to Quran, we need to behave in accordance with our values, rather than what we think, since our thinking is always prone to deficits.

Allah says in the Quran:

But perhaps you hate a thing and it is good for you; and perhaps you love a thing and it is bad for you. And Allah Knows, while you know not. (2:216)

Living in accordance with our values often involves changing the way we act. And it may not be easy. We have strong habits and some of them can hold us back when we try to do things in a different way. Our familiar habits and routines are usually in our comfort zone and moving out of that comfort zone to do something new or different may feel anxious, stressful, and scary. So we often continue as usual, but if we stay in our safe zone, we will never expand the scope of our activities. And as a result, we might miss many opportunities to make our life more interesting and fulfilling. We therefore have the choice of simply doing what feels comfortable to us or to do something new.

If you decide to do something new and stimulating, your mind will probably try to weaken you and warn you. 'You can never do it, also doing this is unnecessary. Don't even worry about it. You will make a fool of yourself.' But now that you have become wise in your mind, you can appreciate it. You don't have to believe your mind and you don't have to obey your mind. You understand that your mind often lets you down and can cause you a lot of grief. So far, your mind may have had too much strength and influence on you and you may well have suffered as a result. So now is a good time to say to your mind what you think: 'I will take charge from now on.' This is your declaration of independence.

When you take control your mind will stay keep on muttering in the background, judging, criticizing, trying to undermine you, but you can just notice it and keep doing what you decide is best. Make a wise decision on the best thing to do, then do the best thing. Don't do anything just because, 'it's what I've always done, and it is the easiest option. It's what my mind tells me to do.' Taking control of your actions will give you a lot more flexibility. When you think hard about what to do and then make a commitment to do it, you go from senseless action to conscious action, from simple reacting to a response. When we have an instant and automatic reaction without thinking, we don't consider the possible alternative actions and we don't make any choices, but a conscious mindful response involves considering different possible actions which is why it increases flexibility. Greater flexibility will open up new opportunities to make your life more interesting, more exciting, more meaningful. and more fulfilling.

Allah guides, by His Blessings, whomever He wills, of those who seek the truth in this Ummah, for success and good direction are from Allah.

This is the conclusion of this book; therefore all that is righteous (in it) comes from Allah, Alone, and all that is evil (in it) comes from the author and Shaitaan.

I ask Allah to make this effort sincere, seeking His Pleasure, and I ask Him to grant us refuge in Him from the evils within us, and that in our actions. I ask him to grant us success in doing what pleases him; He is close and responsive (to the prayers of his faithful servants).